THE PRACTICAL APPLICATIONS OF

# ONE-STEP
# SPARRING

in KARATE-KUNG FU-TAE KWON DO

YOUNG'S TRADING CO.
5705 TELEGRAPH AVE.
OAKLAND, CA 94609
*Complete Martial Art Supplies*

# THE PRACTICAL APPLICATIONS OF
# ONE-STEP SPARRING
## in KARATE-KUNG FU-TAE KWON DO

## by Shin Duk Kang

©Ohara Publications, Incorporated 1978
All rights reserved
Printed in the United States of America
Library of Congress Catalog Card Number: 78-60159
*Fifth Printing 1980*
ISBN No. 0-89750-057-1
*Interior Graphic Design by David Paul Kaplan*

## OHARA 🄾 PUBLICATIONS, INCORPORATED
### BURBANK, CALIFORNIA

# DEDICATION

I am dedicating this book to my mentor in the martial arts, Master Moon Ku Baek, who, through the long years never hesitated to sacrifice his own time and energy, and always looked after me as his own brother. This book is also dedicated to my mother, my wife Jean, my daughter Sheri-Ann and son David.

# ACKNOWLEDGEMENTS

I would like to express my sincere thanks to my student Frank DiMatteo who assisted me in demonstrating the one-step fighting techniques for the pictures in this book and helped to make this book possible, to Denise Pesta and Ann Burkes for helping to edit and arrange the material to prepare it for publication and to Ed Ikuta for his excellent photography.

# ABOUT THE AUTHOR

Like a dervish, Shin Duk Kang whirls in the air, the snap of his flashing, white-uniformed limbs reverberating like the crack of a whip. Then, with devastating speed and deadly accuracy, he targets his opponent with an explosive spinning back kick.

There is both power and grace in his style. Kang is a master warrior and a master artist as well. Each movement melts imperceptibly into the next, and the many, minute motions combine into an ultimately successful fighting style even as many small streams flow into one great river.

But there is another side to this modern warrior. Kang is a dynamic fighter but a patient instructor as well.

His students are both awed by his indomitable fighting skills and inspired by his unceasing dedication to the development of the martial arts.

Kang is a man open to change. He is ready to improvise in his teaching so that his students fulfill their highest potentials. He is willing to investigate new ideas, because he views the martial arts as living, developing arts.

Such devotion must originate in childhood. When Kang was only nine years old, he began to study the martial arts in his native city of Seoul.

For nine years, Kang underwent intensive training in the Korean schools. Martial arts became his world as he led the rigorous life of a student, striving toward self-discipline and self-knowledge.

The first in a series of uprootings came in 1964. Kang's family migrated west, moving to Bolivia. There Kang discovered that his devotion to the martial arts could be combined with a new love—that of teaching what he knew to others. In Kang there was a perfect marriage of skill developed through training and the ability to transmit his knowledge to others. So, after almost a decade of study, Kang first became a teacher of the martial arts.

In Bolivia he taught members of the police academy of La Paz. Then, two years later, his family determined upon another move—this time to the United States.

Kang was the first member of his family to arrive. He settled in Denver and there, overcoming poverty and a language barrier, he worked to help the rest of his family to finance their move to the United States, and he succeeded in earning a grant to attend the University of Colorado.

While completing a B.S. in mechanical engineering, Kang still found time to pursue his lifelong love of the martial arts—again as a teacher. He founded a tae kwon do club at the University of Colorado, and its membership grew from five to 200 members in a single year. He taught TKD to students at the Air Force Academy of Colorado Springs. And he opened his first school in Denver in 1969.

After Kang received his bachelor's degree in 1971, there came another uprooting. This time he moved to Pittsburgh. Again he confronted the familiar problem of having to make a new start in a new place. But, as always, he met his difficulties head-on.

He made his own opportunities by canvassing local YMCAs and YWCAs to institute courses in the martial arts. Within three months, he was able to open his first school in Pittsburgh. It was the beginning of an empire.

More schools followed, and today Kang operates a network of schools in the Pittsburgh area. He also owns several other small businesses, but, as always, the martial arts are his first love.

From his days as a student, Kang noted his insights about the development of his martial arts abilities. As a teacher, he noticed that certain methods were more effective in eliciting rapid progress from his students, and he began to compile ideas concerning his teaching methods. Then, four years ago, he perceived that what had begun as notes had evolved into a systematic approach to fighting techniques.

He began to prepare a guide on his methods for students everywhere. And this first volume is one of the results of his efforts.

# CONTENTS

# INTRODUCTION

## WHAT ARE ONE-STEP FIGHTING TECHNIQUES?

One-step fighting techniques are prearranged attacking and defending movements which are performed in concert by two participants. Students pair off, and one employs various combinations of blocking and counterattacking techniques against the other's punching or kicking attacks.

One-step fighting techniques are among the best methods of familiarizing students with punching, kicking, blocking and all other basic movements. They develop students' aptitudes for rapid and accurate counterattacks, for moving at the right time to the opponent's right vital spot. Because of their effectiveness in developing student skills, they are essential preparation for free-fighting activities.

## WHY ARE ONE-STEP FIGHTING TECHNIQUES IMPORTANT TRAINING IN THE MARTIAL ARTS?

In the United States, there are probably millions of people who practice some form of the martial arts and thousands of schools devoted to the arts of self-defense. These schools encompass a broad range of styles, and each style has its own training methods and ways of executing certain techniques. But within these various forms and styles of the martial arts, one-step fighting techniques are among the most widely-used training methods; they are considered vital training areas in tae kwon do, karate, kung fu and hapkido.

But, up to now, there has been no standard training schedule for these techniques. A beginner learns the appropriate form, (hyung, kata), but what one-step fighting techniques are appropriate to his level? And what techniques are suitable for more advanced students?

There is a need for a systemization of one-step fighting techniques, for a categorization of the techniques according to their complexity which matches them with student levels of advancement in the martial arts. This book attempts to fill this need.

## NOTE TO THE READER

Thirty one-step fighting techniques are presented in this book. Of course, hundreds of combinations and variations can result from each of the techniques introduced, but I do not intend to enumerate all of these possibilities. Rather, each technique presented is meant to embody the countless variations, to be a prototype representing a wide range of possibilities. In this way, each technique should be considered a basic one which students can themselves adapt and use efficiently during freefighting.

This book explains the different methods of beginning one-step fighting techniques as practiced in various schools and styles. But, for convenience and practicality, I have used the parallel ready stance as the starting position.

I hope that what I have written will prove valuable to all those seeking to follow the martial arts and that it will contribute to the unification of all martial arts.

## SUGGESTED TRAINING AND TEACHING SCHEDULE

To develop effective freefighting techniques, one must first gain a solid knowledge of the various techniques utilized in freefighting and be able to perform the best techniques possible for each situation.

This book is designed to familiarize students with various techniques that are effective in freefighting, and may be used as a textbook by instructors in various styles or schools or as a training aid by individual students.

For best results in practicing or teaching the techniques in this book, the following practice schedule is suggested:

| Techniques | Rank |
|---|---|
| 1 through 5 | White Belt |
| 6 through 10 | 8th and 7th Gup (Kyu) |
| 11 through 15 | 6th and 5th Gup (Kyu) |
| 16 through 20 | 4th and 3rd Gup (Kyu) |
| 21 through 25 | 2nd Gup (Kyu) |
| 26 through 30 | 1st Gup (Kyu) |

The above schedule may be adapted in accordance with one's proficiency in the martial arts. And, of course, these one-step fighting techniques should be practiced in accompaniment with appropriate basic movements and forms.

## HOW TO USE THIS BOOK EFFECTIVELY

1. Familiarize yourself with the overall purpose of the book by scanning it page-by-page.

2. Study and practice basic movements and stances presented in this book until you can perform them accurately and without effort. At first, practice slowly and easily, concentrating upon good form and posture. When you can perform the movements correctly, begin practicing with greater power and speed, gradually perfecting them.

3. Practice all kicking and punching techniques as depicted in the illustrations.

4. Now you are prepared to practice the one-step fighting techniques. Find a partner, preferably one of your own rank or ability, and begin practicing the techniques in the order in which they are presented.

5. At first, practice each motion separately and slowly. When you have familiarized yourself with the sequences, you can combine them and begin to practice with greater speed and power.

# STRIKING
# AND BLOCKING POINTS

It is very important to know the striking and blocking points of the body and to select them appropriately. Focusing the strength of the entire body upon these points must be practiced for the best results in defending and attacking.

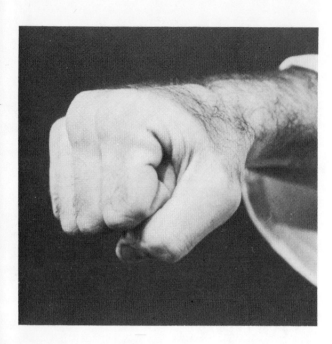

## FOREFIST

The knuckles of the forefinger and the middle finger are used to make contact with the object or opponent. The forefist is the most widely used attacking tool in the martial arts.

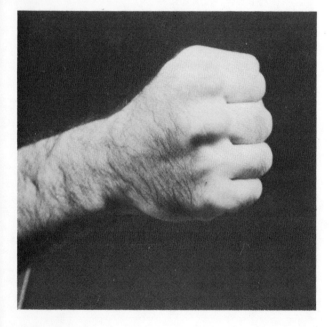

## BACK FIST

The back fist uses the back part of the knuckles of the fore and middle fingers. It is primarily employed for attacking the head area.

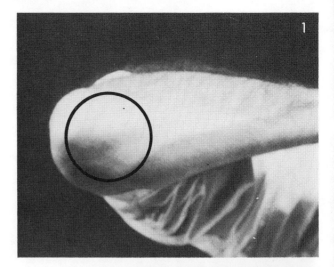

## ELBOW

Three points of the elbow area are used to strike the opponent in close fighting: (1) Front part of elbow, (2) Tip of elbow, (3) Back of elbow.

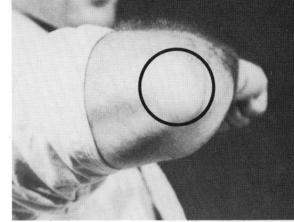

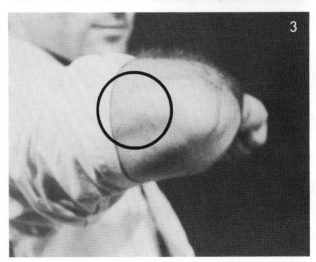

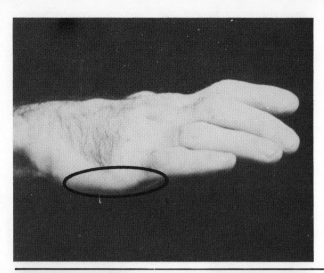

## KNIFEHAND

The knifehand utilizes the edge of the open hand that is opposite the thumb. This striking tool is effective for attacking to the side.

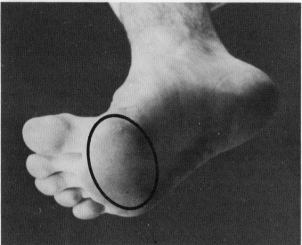

## BALL
## OF THE FOOT

When the ankle is straight and the toes are bent sharply upward, the ball of the foot protrudes to provide good contact. This is used mainly for front and roundhouse kicks.

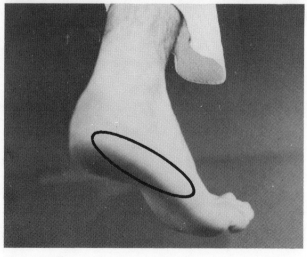

## SIDE
## OF THE FOOT

With toes bent upward and foot pointing slightly downward, the side of the foot is used in side kicks.

## KNEE

The kneecap area is very strong and solid when the knee is sharply bent. This is used for close fighting.

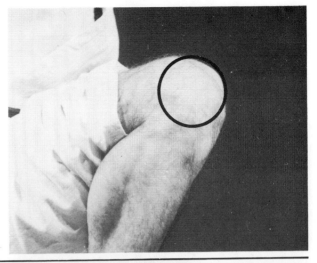

## INSTEP

When attacking the side of a round target, the instep is effective in striking at or beyond the target's center. The instep is one of the striking points of the front and roundhouse kicks.

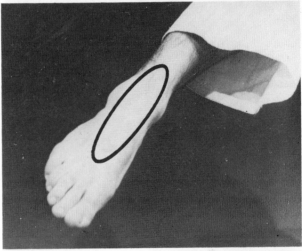

## HEEL

When the toes are bent upward and the foot is bent forward from the ankle, the heel is an effective striking tool in back and spinning wheel kicks.

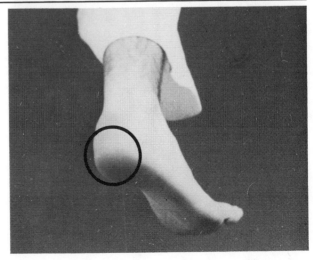

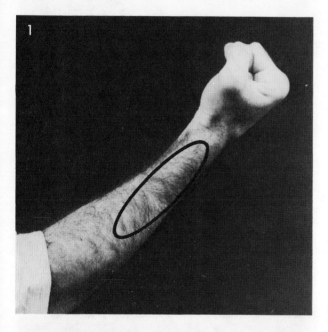

# FOREARM

With the arm bent at the elbow, the hand forms a fist, and the outer and inner forearms are used to block kicks and hand strikes.

(1) Inner forearm,
(2) Outer forearm.

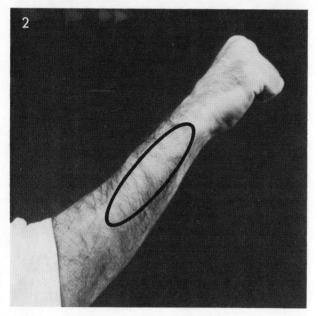

## KNIFEHAND

For the knifehand, the hand is open and fingers are close together and extended. In blocking, the arm is bent at the elbow. Because of the extensive blocking area from the hand to the elbow, the knifehand is the most widely used blocking tool in the martial arts.

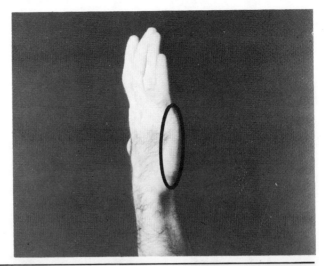

## KNIFE-FOOT

With the ankle and toes bent backward, the outside edge of the foot is used to block and to divert the attack.

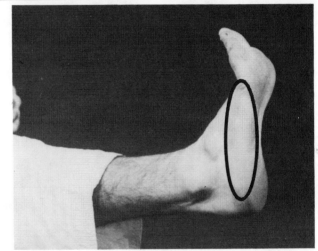

## BOTTOM OF THE FOOT

With the foot tilted slightly inward, the inner edge of the foot is used for blocking and diverting attacks.

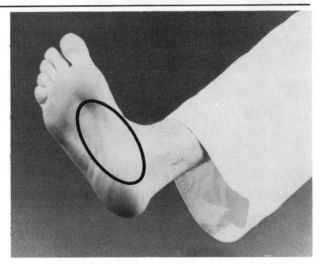

# BASIC MOVEMENTS

The importance of strong, basic striking and blocking techniques begins with the proper stance, progressing to the efficiency and rapidity of the hand techniques and moving to the power and longer striking range of foot techniques.

## STANCES

Strong striking techniques and effective blocking techniques are derived from correct stances. Without correct stances, there can be no good balance; without good balance, there can be no good techniques, power or speed. Stances are the foundation of your techniques. Build a good foundation.

**FRONT VIEW**

## PARALLEL STANCE

Sometimes called the ready stance, this is the beginning position and the stance which is resumed after the execution of a technique or series of movements. Both legs are straight, with feet placed shoulder-width apart and with toes pointed forward. The arms are slightly bent, with hands closed and held about 10 inches away from the body. The body should be loose and posture relaxed during this stance.

**SIDE VIEW**

**FRONT VIEW**

# FORWARD STANCE

The forward leg is bent at the knee, and the back leg is straight and extended, with about 60 percent of the body's weight supported by the front leg. This stance is commonly used for practicing blocking, punching and kicking with the back leg, providing good balance and the source of powerful techniques. But because of the vulnerability of the front area, it is infrequently used in free-fighting. One exception is for lunge and reverse punches. Because the stance provides a long forward range and a solid balance for backing punches, it is particularly effective for these techniques.

**SIDE VIEW**

## BACK STANCE

The upper body should be turned to the side and the knees should be bent, with the rear leg supporting about 70 percent of the body's weight. The rear shoulder may be turned forward about 30 percent to provide better mobility for the rear leg or arm. In many styles of the martial arts, this position is used as a freefighting stance because it increases flexibility of body movement and a smaller front target area is accessible to the opponent.

**FRONT VIEW**

**SIDE VIEW**

**FRONT VIEW**

# STRADDLE STANCE

The upper body is straight, and the legs are bent at the knees with the body's weight equally distributed. This stance is generally used for both front-facing and side-facing attacks and blocks. For side-facing techniques, the stance is a very good defensive move because it provides solid balance and only a small target area is accessible to the opponent. This position is also used as a training stance for many hand techniques, because of the good sideways balance it engenders.

**SIDE VIEW**

## FIGHTING STANCE

The fighting stance is actually any stance which permits freedom of movement. The hands are placed in front of the body for blocking or attacking easily and properly. They should be positioned to act effectively as guards against kicks and punches as well as striking weapons for quick counterattacks. The hands will not obstruct the view of the opponent if they are placed below eye level. Since it is preferred by a majority of martial artists, the back stance has been selected as the fighting stance to illustrate the techniques in this book.

**FRONT VIEW**

**SIDE VIEW**

29

## HAND TECHNIQUES

Hand techniques are efficient because of the rapidity with which they can be performed.

They are of two types: offensive and defensive—striking and blocking.

An effective attack is contingent upon perceiving an accessible target and selecting the correct striking tool. In many cases a hand technique is best because of the speed with which a strike can be delivered. It must be performed with a concentration of speed, strength, good stance and posture.

An effective block involves the recognition and instantaneous parrying of an offensive strike. Although in some cases foot techniques are used defensively, hands are the principal mode of blocking.

## LUNGE PUNCH

(1) This punch is performed from a forward stance and is executed by the right hand if the right leg is extended forward, and (2) the left hand if it is the left leg that is advanced. (3) The other arm is extended before the punch and is retracted at the moment of the strike. (4) The punching fist is held, palm-side up, close to the side. The strike is made in a straight line to the target, with the wrist twisting the fist palm-side down immediately before impact. The shoulders should be relaxed but the punching fist tightly clenched. Twisting the waist and hip sharply as the punch is delivered will put the force of the entire body behind the strike and maximize snapping power.

## REVERSE PUNCH

(1 & 2) The reverse punch is performed from a forward stance and utilizes the same motions as the lunge punch. It differs only in the arm that makes the strike being

executed by the right hand if the left leg is extended forward (3), and by the left hand if it is the right leg that is advanced (4).

FRONT OF THE ELBOW

## ELBOW (THREE SIDES)

Elbow attacks are highly effective for close fighting, and three different parts of the elbow can be used: (1&2) When the outside of the forearm arcs toward the target, the front of the elbow is used for the strike. (3&4) When the bent arm moves directly toward the opponent, the tip of the elbow is used for the strike. (5&6) When the back of the upper arm arcs toward the target, the back of the elbow is used for the strike.

TIP OF THE ELBOW

BACK OF THE ELBOW

1

2

## FORWARD CHOP

(1) The forward chop, which is depicted being delivered from a forward stance, (2) uses the knife-hand in attacking mainly the side of the neck, the temple or the midsection. (3&4) From behind the ear, the striking hand

3

slices forward in a circular motion, with the hand twisting palm-upward just before contact. For balance and power, the other hand is drawn back to the side in a palm-upward fist at the moment of the strike.

4

## BACKWARD CHOP

The backward chop, (1) shown from a straddle stance, (2) uses the knife-hand as the striking point.

(3) To begin, the palm is turned toward the face. (4) The striking hand slices toward the target with the palm turning downward just before impact.

The backward chop can be performed from all stances.

**APPLICATION**

## SIDE PUNCH

This punch, (1) delivered from a straddle stance, possesses the dual advantage of safety and effectiveness; while displaying no directly accessible target area to the opponent, it permits a strike of considerable range.

(2-4) The punching fist is originally positioned slightly behind the waist, facilitating the delivery of the strike in a straight line to the target.

The side punch can also be delivered from a back stance.

**APPLICATION**

## BACK FIST

This strike, (1) delivered from a straddle stance, uses the first two knuckles as the striking point.

(2) The arm is drawn back above the opposite shoulder, which, (3&4) combining with the motion of the waist and hip, increases the power of the strike.

The back fist is widely used in freefighting because it can be delivered with greater speed than most other strikes. The attack has good smashing power and, if properly used, can be devastating.

The back fist can also be delivered from a back stance.

## DOWNWARD
## BLOCK

This technique, (1) delivered from a forward stance, is effective in blocking an opponent's kick or hand strike to the abdomen or groin area.

(2&3) The arms are crossed with the blocking arm on top. (4) This arm

3

executes a sweeping block with the fist twisting immediately before completion, while the other arm is simultaneously retracted to the side.

The downward block can be executed from any stance.

**SIDE VIEW**

4

## OUTWARD BLOCK (OPEN AND CLOSED HAND)

This technique, (1) delivered from a forward stance, is used to stop a strike to the chest, neck or lower face area, and it utilizes the outer forearm or knifehand as the blocking point.

(2&3) In preparation, the arms are crossed with the blocking arm on top;

3

this strengthens the force of the block and helps to guard the vital points that are under attack.

(4) The block should be directed to the opponent's striking wrist or ankle.

The outward block can be performed from almost any stance.

**SIDE VIEW**

4

## INWARD BLOCK

This technique, (1) delivered from a forward stance, is usually used to block the opponent's attack to the wrist or ankle.

(2&3) The arm is initially drawn to the side, the hand level with the head. (4) The closed or open hand is swept across the body with the

**3**

wrist being sharply twisted just before completion. The blocking arm should not sweep beyond the opposite shoulder in order to maintain an effective guard and good balance.

The inward block can be executed from all stances.

**SIDE VIEW**

**4**

1

2

## UPWARD BLOCK

This technique, (1) delivered from a forward stance, uses the outer forearm or knifehand as the blocking point to protect the head.

(2) In preparation, the arms should be crossed with the blocking arm on top. (3&4) Rising motion

3

should propel the arm above the head, and the wrist should be tilted to a 45-degree angle to utilize the outer forearm with maximum effectiveness.

The upward block can also be delivered from a back stance.

**SIDE VIEW**

4

1

## CIRCLE
## WRIST BLOCK

This block, (1&2) delivered from a back stance, utilizes the inner forearm as the blocking point. (3) Initially the arms are palms down and parallel a few inches apart; they are crossed in front of the body with the blocking arm underneath.

2

3

(4) The blocking arm arcs upward and outward, with the wrist twisting immediately before completion for maximum snap.

The circle wrist block can also be delivered from a forward stance.

**SIDE VIEW**

4

1

## DOUBLE KNIFE-HAND BLOCK

This block, (1) delivered from a back stance, utilizes the knifehand or the outer forearm as the blocking point. (2) Both arms are drawn back and to one side, with the blocking hand angled palm upward and the other hand angled palm

2

3

downward. (3&4) Both hands rotate in a slight circular motion and must be turned at the moment of impact. The blocking hand sweeps across the face to deflect the strike while the other hand is simultaneously brought to the solar plexus.

SIDE VIEW

4

## FOOT TECHNIQUES

Foot techniques are efficient because they are delivered with greater power than hand techniques, and because they encompass a further striking range. Like hand techniques, they can be used both offensively and defensively, but they are almost exclusively employed for striking.

The knee is of primary importance in the delivery of an effective kick. For the kick to have "snap," the knee must be bent initially and then fully extended at the moment of impact.

## FRONT KICK

(1) This kick is an effective striking technique to the groin, midsection or high section. The ball of the foot is the primary striking point. However, the instep is highly effective in attacks to the groin. (2) The supporting leg is bent slightly at the knee. The kicking leg is sharply bent, with that foot suspended near the stationary knee. (3&4) The kick can be performed with either a snapping or thrusting motion, with the latter employing more power from the hip. The snap kick has superior breaking power, while the thrust kick has more pushing power.

## SIDE KICK

The side kick, (1) utilizing the back half of the side of the foot, is one of the most frequently used kicks in all styles of karate because of its great range and force.

(2) The kicking leg must be bent sharply with the foot brought alongside the stationary knee. (3) The waist twists and the hip pushes the kick in a straight motion from the knee of the stationary leg to the target.

While there are diverse methods of executing the side kick, (4) depicted is the turning side kick in which the back leg is used for the strike.

## ROUNDHOUSE KICK

(1&2) This kick, utilizing the ball of the foot or the instep as the striking point, is ideal for attacking an opponent from the side.

(3) In preparation, the kicking leg is bent sharply at the knee and drawn to one side. The calf should be almost parallel with the floor. (4&5) The kick is snapped to the target in a semicircular motion.

## KNEE

(1) The knee is an effective close-distance technique used on the groin, (2) the midsection or the face—especially when the opponent's upper body is bent forward. The knee must be thrust sharply from the hip for maximum power.

## SPINNING
## WHEEL KICK

The spinning wheel kick, utilizing the heel as the striking point, is extremely powerful because of its momentum.

(1) When initiated from a fighting stance, this kick begins with the front foot being turned inward and the rear leg being raised.

(2) During execution, the front foot turns 180 degrees, (3&4) spinning the body sharply. (5&6) The kicking leg straightens at the moment of contact and, to avoid blind attack, the head should be turned to sight the target before carrying through the strike.

## SPINNING BACK KICK

The spinning back kick utilizes the back half of the side of the foot as the striking point.

(1 & 2) The initial motion is similar to that of the spinning wheel kick since the front foot is turned inward and the rear leg is elevated. (3) The kicking leg is bent sharply at the knee with the foot brought alongside the stationary knee. (4) During execution, the striking foot moves in a straight line from the stationary knee to the target.

As in the spinning wheel kick, a blind attack should be avoided by sighting the target before carrying through the strike.

## SPINNING CRESCENT KICK

The spinning crescent kick utilizes the side of the foot as the striking point to attack the target from the side.

(1—3) Initially, the front foot turns inward and the kicking rear foot is bent sharply. (4) During execution, the front foot turns nearly full-circle, while the kicking leg is snapped just before impact.

As in all spinning kicks, a blind attack should be avoided by sighting the target just before carrying through the strike.

## JUMP FRONT KICK

The jump front kick utilizes the ball of the foot in upward or forward strikes against high target areas.

(1) The front leg, which propels the jump, is slightly bent at the knee. (2) The other leg is drawn up alongside the front knee and is pulled higher during the jump to increase the height of the jump. (3) The jumping leg passes the other leg in a scissors-like motion, bending and snapping to execute the kick.

The kicking foot should follow the other foot in landing as lightly as possible to maintain good balance.

## JUMP SIDE KICK

(1) The jump side kick utilizes the back half of the side of the foot as the striking point against high target areas.

This kick differs from the jump front kick because the leg that executes the kick is not the leg that propels the jump. (2) The rear foot is brought alongside the knee of the front leg which propels the jump. (3) When the jump occurs, the jumping leg is pulled up and tucked under the other leg as the body turns in the direction of the target. (4&5) At the zenith of the jump, the kicking leg snaps open to complete the strike in the same manner as in a turning side kick.

The kicking leg follows the other leg in landing, which must be done lightly and with good balance.

## JUMP ROUNDHOUSE KICK

(1) This kick, utilizing the ball of the foot or the instep as the striking point, is ideal for attacking high targets from the side. (2) Both legs are bent at the knees to propel the jump, with the leg that will execute the kick in the rear position. (3) After the jump, the body turns in the air in the direction of the target, and the leg that was originally in the front position is tucked under the body. (4) The kicking leg snaps into the target with a semicircular motion.

The jump roundhouse kick is often performed with only one leg propelling the jump; the front leg jumps and also executes the strike.

## JUMP CRESCENT KICK

The jump crescent kick utilizes the side of the foot as the striking point to attack high targets from the side.

(1&2) Both legs are bent to propel the jump, with the foot that will execute the kick in back of the other foot. (3) After the jump, the body turns 180 degrees in the air, the direction depending upon the foot that was originally in the rear; if the right foot was back, the body should turn to the right. (4) The kicking leg should remain bent until the moment before impact to achieve good snapping power.

# TARGET AREAS

It is necessary to practice striking vital points rather than delivering blows to a general area. A prerequisite for striking vital spots is a knowledge of their exact locations, and much practice is needed to pinpoint them accurately every time.

Although countless points on the anatomy are vulnerable to attack, this book has focused upon those target areas against which strikes are most frequently directed in freefighting.

TEMPLE

FACE
(for high-section attack)

SOLAR PLEXUS
(for midsection attack)

STOMACH
(for midsection attack)

GROIN
(for low-section attack)

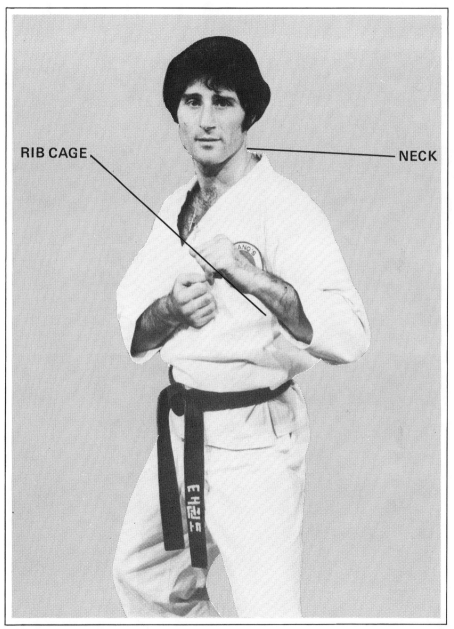

RIB CAGE

NECK

# DIFFERENT WAYS OF BEGINNING ONE-STEP FIGHTING TECHNIQUES

In the many styles of the martial arts, various methods are used to begin one-step fighting techniques. In this book, for convenience and practicality, the parallel ready stance is always used as the beginning stance for both fighters. However, in this section I am including illustrations of the five most commonly used beginning positions; according to their styles, students can select one of these five positions to substitute for the parallel ready stance in beginning the techniques.

**POSITION 1**

A: Parallel Stance
B: Parallel Stance

## POSITION 2

A: Fighting Stance
B: Fighting Stance

## POSITION 3

A: Fighting Stance
B: Parallel Stance

## POSITION 4

A: Forward Stance
B: Parallel Stance

**POSITION 5**

A: Forward Stance
B: Fighting Stance

## REVERSE PUNCH IN ONE-STEP FIGHTING

The reverse punch may be substituted for the lunge punch in all one-step fighting techniques. (1—3) However, when a reverse punch is executed, only starting stances should be used.

# ONE-STEP FIGHTING TECHNIQUES

The student who has studied the preceding sections on striking and blocking points and who has practiced the attacking and defending techniques is ready to begin the one-step fighting techniques.

For all techniques, the attacking fighter is designated A, and the defending and counterattacking fighter is designated B.

The attacking fighter should always precede his offensive move—which will always be a lunge punch—with a yell. The defending fighter should always signal his readiness to block and counterattack with a yell.

The attacking fighter should always keep his punching arm extended until the defending fighter has executed all of the blocking and counterattacking movements specified. He should then signal his completion of the blocking and counterattacking sequence with a yell.

At the conclusion of each technique, although it is not indicated in the illustrations, both fighters should always return to their original stances at the same time.

Finally, although the illustrations always depict the attacking fighter executing a right-handed strike, students should, of course, practice on both right and left sides.

| For All Techniques: |
| --- |
| Ready Stance: Parallel Ready Stance<br><br>       A: Person Initiating the Attack<br>       B: Person Blocking and Counterattacking |

## TECHNIQUE ONE

(1) From a ready position, (2&3) step forward with the left foot into a left forward stance, execute a closed-hand outward block with the left hand. (4) Right high reverse punch, (5) left lunge punch to midsection. (6) Return to ready position.

Note: As indicated in the introduction to this section, A always executes a lunge punch as his offensive move. B then performs all the blocking and counterattacking movements listed under each technique.

## TECHNIQUE TWO

(1) Stepping forward with the left foot into a left forward stance, execute a left upward block; (2—4) grab A's arm with the left hand.*

Use a right high re-

verse punch*, and a (5) right knee kick to stomach or groin.

*Steps 2 and 3 are performed simultaneously.

## TECHNIQUE THREE

(1) From a ready position, (2—6) step forward with the right foot into a straddle stance. Execute a right inward open-hand block; right chop to the neck, (7) pulling back the right hand, using the tip of the elbow to execute a strike to the solar plexus. Push the right fist with the left hand to add power to the strike.

**OPPOSITE SIDE VIEW**

## TECHNIQUE FOUR

(1) From a ready position, (2) step forward 45 degrees with the right foot into a right forward stance; (3) execute a left reverse punch to the solar plexus. (4&5) Pulling the left hand back to the right shoulder, exe-

3

cute a left open-hand
outward block while piv-
oting into a left forward
stance*; high reverse
punch with right fist.*

---

*Steps 2 and 3 are
performed simultaneous-
ly.

4

5

B    A

## TECHNIQUE FIVE

(1) From a ready position, (2) step back with the right foot into a left forward stance, (3) for a right front kick to the solar plexus. (4&5) Stepping down into a 45-degree right straddle stance,

perform a left open-hand
outward block and simul-
taneously deliver a right
high punch; (6) left re-
verse punch to the mid-
section while twisting
into a right forward
stance.

## TECHNIQUE SIX

(1) From a ready position, (2&3) step forward with the right foot into a right straddle stance and execute a right inward open-hand block. (4—6) Using the tip of the right elbow, execute a strike to the solar plexus, followed by a (7) right hammerfist to the groin.

## TECHNIQUE SEVEN

(1) From a ready position, (2&3) with the right foot, step across A's right leg into a right straddle stance as you execute a right open-hand inward block. (4&5) Using the back of the right elbow, execute a strike to the rib cage. (6&7) Turning to the left, use the back of the left elbow to strike the solar plexus.

## TECHNIQUE EIGHT

(1) From the ready position, (2&3) with the left foot, step across A's right leg into a left straddle stance as you execute a left open-hand inward block, (4) a right reverse punch to the rib cage as you twist into a left forward stance, (5&6) a left reverse punch to the face as you twist into a right forward stance, and (7) a right open-hand forward chop to the solar plexus as you again twist into a left forward stance.

## TECHNIQUE NINE

(1—3) Remaining in a ready position, execute a right inward open-hand block. (4&5) Stepping forward with the left foot into a left straddle stance, execute a high side punch. (6&7) Spinning to the right and sliding the right foot closer to A, use the back of the elbow for a strike to the solar plexus.

2

4

5

7

**OPPOSITE SIDE VIEW**

A          B

## TECHNIQUE TEN

(1) From the ready position, (2) step back with the right foot into a left forward stance, dropping both fists to the sides. (3&4) Execute a right turning side kick to the midsection. (5&6) Stepping into a right straddle stance,

use the right hand to deliver an inward open-hand block; (7) right backward chop to the neck and (8) while sliding the right foot sideways shift into a right forward stance, executing a left reverse punch to the midsection.

## TECHNIQUE ELEVEN

(1) Start from the ready position and, (2 & 3) stepping forward with the left foot, execute a left circle wrist block from a left back stance. (4) Sliding the left foot sideways to shift into a left forward

stance, grab A's right wrist as you deliver a right reverse punch to the midsection. (5) Sliding the right foot forward next to the left foot, use the front of the right elbow for an upward strike to the face.

## TECHNIQUE TWELVE

(1) From the ready position, (2—4) with the left foot step across A's right leg into a left straddle stance as you execute a left open-hand inward block; (5&6) right open-hand forward chop to the solar plexus as you twist into a left forward stance, and (7&8) a left chop to the back of the neck, pushing A's head down as you twist into a right forward stance. (9) Twisting back into a left forward stance, use the back of the right elbow to deliver a downward strike to the spine.

## TECHNIQUE THIRTEEN

(1) From the ready position, (2—4) step forward 45 degrees with the right foot into a right straddle stance as you deliver a left open-hand outward block and a right open-hand forward chop to the neck. (5) Twisting into a left forward stance, use the front of the right elbow for a strike to the temple. (6&7) Twisting back into a straddle stance, use the back of the right elbow for attacking the face.

# TECHNIQUE FOURTEEN

(1) From a ready position, (2&3) with the left foot, step across A's right leg into a left forward stance as you execute a right openhand outward block to A's outside wrist. (4&5) Grab A's wrist and execute a right roundhouse kick to the solar plexus, then (6&7) step into a right forward stance, left reverse punch to the rib cage.

## TECHNIQUE FIFTEEN

(1) Starting from the ready position, (2&3) step back with the right foot into a left fighting stance, following with a (4&5) right roundhouse kick to the temple. (6&7) Stepping down into a right straddle stance, execute an inward open-hand block and (8) a right backward chop to the neck. (9) Sliding the right foot sideways to shift into a right forward stance, execute a left reverse punch to the midsection.

110

## TECHNIQUE
## SIXTEEN

(1) From the ready position, (2&3) step forward with the left foot into a left back stance and execute a left double knifehand block. (4) Sliding the left foot sideways to shift into a left forward stance, deliver a right reverse punch

to the midsection while keeping the left hand in an open-hand blocking position. (5) Grab A's head with both hands. (6) While pulling A's head down, execute a strike to the face with the right knee.

## TECHNIQUE SEVENTEEN

(1) From the ready position, (2&3) with the left foot, step across A's right leg into a left straddle stance while executing a right open-hand outward block to his outside wrist. (4&5) Grab A's wrist and deliver a side kick to the rib cage. (6—8) Stepping down from the side kick, execute a right foot sweep to the back of A's right foot, and (9) twisting into a right forward stance, follow with a left reverse punch to the face.

## TECHNIQUE EIGHTEEN

(1) From a ready position, (2&3) with the left foot, step across A's right leg into a left straddle stance as you execute a left open-hand inward block, pushing A's hand downward. (4) Twisting into a left forward stance, bring the right hand upward near the left and grab A's right hand with both hands. (5) Twist A's hand towards his back. (6&7) As A loses balance, continue twisting his hands backwards, and deliver a side kick to the back of his knee.

116

## TECHNIQUE NINETEEN

(1) Starting at the ready position, (2&3) step back with the right foot into a left fighting stance and (4—6) execute a right spinning back kick to the face. Stepping down into a right forward stance, (7) deliver a left reverse punch to the solar plexus.

## TECHNIQUE TWENTY

(1) From the ready position, (2&3) with the left foot step across A's right leg into a left forward stance while executing a right outward open-hand block to A's outside wrist, followed by a (4&5) right side kick to the rib cage. (6—9) Stepping the right foot down by the left, execute a left spinning wheel kick to the midsection or the face area.

## TECHNIQUE TWENTY-ONE

(1) From the ready position, (2&3) with the left foot step forward into a left forward stance, and while angling the upper body slightly to the left, catch A's arm between your right elbow and biceps. (4) Twisting into a straddle stance, hit the back of A's elbow with the left arm, (5&6) pushing A's arm downward while shifting into a low right forward stance. (7&8) Place A's arm on your right knee and execute a right downward chop to the back of his neck.

## TECHNIQUE TWENTY-TWO

(1) Start at the ready position, and (2—4) with the right foot, step 45 degrees forward into a right straddle stance, simultaneously executing a left outward, open-hand block and a right high punch. (5) Twisting into a right forward stance, execute a left reverse punch to the midsection. (6—8) Stepping forward with the left foot and turning your body clockwise, execute a right open-hand chop to the throat.

## TECHNIQUE
## TWENTY-THREE

(1) From the ready position, (2&3) with the right foot step forward into a right straddle stance while executing a right open-hand inward block, followed by (4&5) a right chop to the neck. (6&7) Sliding into a right forward stance, deliver a left reverse punch to the midsection. (8&9) Twisting into a left forward stance, execute a right reverse punch to the face area,

(CONTINUED)

(CONTINUED ON NEXT PAGE)

127

(10) using the right open-hand to push A's arm. (11—13) Twisting into a right straddle stance again, right backward chop to the neck and follow through with a left reverse punch to the midsection. (14&15) Bring both hands to the right side, and twist into a left forward stance as you simultaneously execute a left open-hand block and a right reverse high punch.

1

## TECHNIQUE TWENTY-FOUR

(1) From the ready position, (2—4) step forward 45 degrees with the right foot into a right straddle stance while simultaneously executing a left open-hand block and a right high punch. (5) Bring A's right arm downward with the right hand, and grab his arm with both hands. (6&7) With the left foot, take a half-step forward, and turn clockwise by moving the right foot backwards while holding A's hand with both hands. (8&9) From the clockwise turn, step into a right forward stance and throw A backwards by simultaneously pulling down his arm and executing a foot sweep with the right leg.

4

7

2

3

5

6

8

9

## TECHNIQUE
## TWENTY-FIVE

(1) From a ready position, (2—4) step forward 45 degrees with the right foot, and execute a thrusting left side kick to the solar plexus. (5—8) As you step down, execute a right spinning, reverse, crescent kick to the face.

## TECHNIQUE TWENTY-SIX

(1) From the ready position, (2&3) with the left foot, step across A's right leg into a left forward stance while executing a right open-hand block to his outside wrist. (4—6) Grab A's wrist and strike the shoulder with a right crescent kick. (7&8) Keeping the right leg in the air, execute a right side kick to the rib cage, then (9—11) step down, and jump with both feet to execute a right jump side kick to the head.

## TECHNIQUE
## TWENTY-SEVEN

(1) From the ready position, (2) with the right foot, step back to shift into a left fighting stance, (3—5) using a right crescent kick to block A's outside wrist. (6&7) Upon stepping down, execute a left front kick to the midsection and (8—10) a right roundhouse kick to the temple.

136

 2

 3

 5

 6

 9

 10

## TECHNIQUE
## TWENTY-EIGHT

(1) From the ready position, (2) step back with the right foot to shift into a left fighting stance. (3—5) With the bottom of the right foot, block A's outside wrist. (6&7) Without stepping down, right side kick to the midsection and (8&9) side kick to the face.

2

3

5

6

8

9

## TECHNIQUE
## TWENTY-NINE

(1) From a ready position, (2) step back with the left foot to shift into a right fighting stance. (3) With the left foot, execute a front snap kick. (4—7) As the left foot steps down, jump with the left foot to execute a left jump front kick to the face, (8—10) landing with the left foot forward, and executing a right jump roundhouse kick to the temple.

## TECHNIQUE THIRTY

(1) From a ready position, (2—4) step forward 45 degrees with the right foot and execute a left thrusting side kick to the solar plexus. (5—8) Stepping down, jump with both feet to execute a right spinning reverse crescent kick to the face.